Pocket

School Yard Jokes

h

hinkler

Published by Hinkler Books Pty Ltd
45–55 Fairchild Street
Heatherton Victoria 3202 Australia
www.hinkler.com.au

© Hinkler Books Pty Ltd 2010

Cover Illustration: Rob Kiely
Illustrations: Glen Singleton
Prepress: Splitting Image
Typesetting: MPS Limited

ISBN: 978 1 7418 5790 0

Printed and bound in China

Contents

Sibling Rivalry

Did you hear about the time Eddie's sister tried to make a birthday cake?

The candles melted in the oven.

My sister went on a crash diet.

Is that why she looks like such a wreck?

Mummy, mummy, Sis has got a bruise.

Shut up and eat around it.

1

What do you call the cannibal who ate her father's sister?

An aunt-eater!

Teacher: *'How was your holiday, Penny?'*

Penny: *'Great. My brother and I spent the whole time on the beach, burying each other in the sand.'*

Teacher: *'That sounds like fun.'*

Penny: *'Daddy says we can go back next year and find him.'*

Why was the boy unhappy to win the prize for best costume at the Halloween party?

Because he just came to pick up his little sister!

First vampire: *'I don't think much of your sister's neck!'*

Second vampire: *'Don't worry, just eat the vegetables.'*

Mother: *'Cathy, get your little sister's hat out of that puddle!'*

Cathy: *'I can't, Mum. She's got it strapped too tight under her chin.'*

Get me out from under here before I drown

Brother: *'What happened to you?'*

Sister: *'I fell off while I was riding.'*

Brother: *'Horseback?'*

Sister: *'I don't know. I'll find out when I get back to the stable.'*

Boy: *'Dad! Dad! Come out – my sister's fighting a 10-foot gargoyle with three heads!'*

Dad: *'No, I'm not coming out. She's going to have to learn to look after herself.'*

James: *'My sister has lovely long hair, all down her back.'*

Will: *'Pity it's not on her head!'*

Why doesn't your sister like peanuts?

Have you ever seen a skinny elephant?

I gave up peanut eating 6 months ago ...now I'm down to a lovely SIZE 10

Why did your sister keep running around her bed?

Because she was trying to catch up on her sleep!

Mary: *'Do you think my sister's pretty?'*

Tim: *'Well, let's just say if you pulled her pigtail, she'd probably say "oink, oink"!'*

My sister is so dim that she thinks a cartoon is something you sing in the car!

Doctor, Doctor, my little brother thinks he's a computer.

Well bring him in so I can cure him.

I can't, I need to use him to finish my homework!

Why did your sister put her socks on inside out?

Because there was a hole on the outside.

Did the bionic monster have a brother?

No, but he had lots of trans-sisters!

Charlie had a puppy on a leash. He met his brother Jim and said, *'I just got this puppy for our little brother.'*

'Really?' said Jim. *'That was good value as a swap!'*

First boy: *'Why is your brother always flying off the handle?'*

Second boy: *'Because he's got a screw loose!'*

First boy: *'My brother said he'd tell me everything he knows.'*

Second boy: *'He must have been speechless!'*

7

Peter: 'My brother wants to work badly!'

Anita: 'As I remember, he usually does!'

Did you hear about the girl who got her brother a birthday cake, but then

couldn't figure out how to get the cake in the typewriter to write 'Happy Birthday'?

My sister is so dumb that she thinks a buttress is a female goat!

Dan: *'My little brother is a real pain.'*

Nan: *'Things could be worse.'*

Dan: *'How?'*

Nan: *'He could be twins!'*

First boy: *'Does your brother keep himself clean?'*

Second boy: *'Oh, yes, he takes a bath every month, whether he needs one or not!'*

Maybe I should bathe a little more regularly than I do...

Mum: *'What are you doing, son?'*

Boy: *'Writing my brother a letter.'*

Mum: *'That's a lovely idea, but why are you writing so slowly?'*

Boy: *'Because he can't read very fast!'*

Little brother: *'I'm going to buy a sea horse.'*

Big brother: *'Why?'*

Little brother: *'Because I want to play water polo!'*

Big brother: *'That planet over there is Mars.'*

Little brother: *'Then that other one must be Pa's.'*

Why did your brother ask your father to sit in the freezer?

Because he wanted an ice-cold pop!

The mother monster asked her son what he was doing with a saw, and if he'd seen his brother.

'You mean my new half-brother, Mummy,' he replied!

Brother: *'Where was Solomon's temple?'*
Sister: *'On either side of his head.'*

Poking Fun at Teachers

Science teacher: *'What are nitrates?'*

Student: *'Cheaper than day rates.'*

English teacher: *'Jamie, give me a sentence beginning with "I".*

Jamie: *'I is …'.*

Teacher: *'No Jamie, you must always say "I am".'*

Jamie: *'Okay. I am the ninth letter of the alphabet.'*

History teacher: *'What's a Grecian urn?'*

Student: *'About $500 a week.'*

What's the difference between a train station and a teacher?

One minds the train, the other trains the mind.

Did you hear about the maths teacher who wanted to order pizza for dinner, but was divided about whether to have additional cheese?

Teacher: *'Did you know the bell had gone?'*
Sue: *'I didn't take it, Miss.'*

History teacher: *'What was Camelot?'*
Student: *'A place where camels are parked.'*

Teacher: 'If I bought 100 buns for a dollar, what would each bun be?'

Student: 'Stale.'

One of those stale old bargain buns that made its way into the teacher's lunchbox

Teacher: 'Wally, why are you late?'

Wally: 'The train had a flat tyre.'

History teacher: 'What's the best thing about history?'

Mary: 'All the dates.'

In which class do you learn how to shop for bargains?

Buy-ology.

'Mary,' said her teacher, 'you can't bring that lamb into class. What about the smell?'

'Oh, that's all right Miss,' replied Mary. 'It'll soon get used to it.'

PHEW! What did you stand in? It smells like you've just come from a farm!

'What are three words most often used by students?' the teacher asked the class.

'I don't know,' sighed a student.

'That's correct!' said the teacher.

Shane: 'Dad, today my teacher yelled at me for something I didn't do.'

Dad: 'What did he yell at you for?'

Shane: 'For not doing my homework.'

When George left school he was going to be a printer.

All his teachers said he was the right type.

Teacher: *'What came after the Stone Age and the Bronze Age?'*

Student: *'The saus-age.'*

Principal: *'You should have been here at 9.00.'*

Student: *'Why, what happened?'*

17

Mother: *'Did you get a good place in the geography test?'*

Daughter: *'Yes, I sat next to the cleverest kid in the class.'*

Teacher: *'That's three times I've asked you a question. Why won't you reply?'*

Student: *'Because you told me not to answer you back.'*

Geography teacher: *'What's the coldest country in the world?'*

Student: *'Chile.'*

How many aerobic teachers does it take to change a light bulb?

Five, one to change it, the others to say, 'A Little to the left, a little to the right, a little to the left, a little to the right.'

History teacher: *'Here is a question to check that you did your homework on British kings and queens. Who came after Mary?'*

Student: *'Her little lamb.'*

I wish we could get out of the Dark Ages! Reading by candlelight is going to send me blind.!! Whats worse is its going to be 900 years before someone invents the lightbulb.

History teacher: *'Why do we refer to the period around 1000 years AD as the Dark Ages?'*

Student: *'Because there were so many knights.'*

When Dad came home, he was amazed to see his son sitting on a horse, writing something. *'What are you doing up there?'* he asked.

'Well, the teacher told us to write an essay on our favourite animal,' replied the boy.

Why did the teacher wear sunglasses?

Because his students were so bright.

Cookery teacher: *'Helen, what are the best things to put in a fruit cake?'*

Helen: *'Teeth!'*

20

Did you hear about the cross-eyed teacher?

He couldn't control his pupils.

Father: *'I want to take my girl out of this terrible maths class.'*

Teacher: *'But she's top of the class!'*

Father: *'That's why it must be a terrible class!'*

Teacher: *'I'd like you to be very quiet today, girls. I've got a dreadful headache.'*

Mary: *'Please Miss, why don't you do what Mum does when she has a headache?'*

Teacher: *'What's that?'*

Mary: *'She sends us out to play!'*

Maths teacher: *'Paul. If you had five pieces of chocolate and Sam asked for one of them, how many would you have left?'*

Paul: *'Five.'*

Teacher: *'I hope I didn't see you copying from John's exam paper, James.'*

James: *'I hope you didn't see me either!'*

What is the robot teacher's favourite part of the day?

Assembly.

What is the easiest way to get a day off school?

Wait until Saturday.

Science teacher: *'Which travels faster, heat or cold?'*

Student: *'Heat, because you can catch a cold.'*

What would you get if you crossed a teacher with a vampire?

Lots of blood tests.

NOW...
YOUR BLOOD TEST
has come back
TYPE A ...
Top marks!

Student to teacher: *'I don't want to worry you but my dad said that if my grades don't improve, someone's going to get a spanking.'*

Teacher: *'What's the name of a liquid that won't freeze?'*
Student: *'Hot water.'*

Teacher: *'Can anyone tell me what the Dog Star is?'*
Student: *'Lassie.'*

Teacher: *'I wish you'd pay a little attention.'*
Student: *'I'm paying as little attention as possible.'*

JONES! JONES! You're not sleeping are you? What's the last letter of the alphabet?

24

Student: *'Would you punish someone for something they didn't do?'*

Teacher: *'Of course not.'*

Student: *'Good, because I didn't do my homework.'*

Teacher: *'Billy, stop making ugly faces at the other students!'*

Billy: *'Why?'*

Teacher: *'Well, when I was your age, I was told that if I kept making ugly faces, my face would stay that way.'*

Billy: *'Well, I can see you didn't listen.'*

Sir...If the wind changes direction we don't stay this way do we?

Have you heard about the gym teacher who ran around exam rooms, hoping to jog students' memories?

. . . Or, the craft teacher who had her pupils in stitches?

. . . Or, maybe, the cookery teacher who thought Hamlet was an omelette with bacon?

Dad: *'How did you find your maths exam?'*
Son: *'Unfortunately, it wasn't lost!'*

What is an English teacher's favourite fruit?
The Grapes of Wrath.

Teacher: *'Why can't you answer any of my questions in class?'*

Student: *'If I could, there wouldn't be much point in me being here.'*

LOST CHILD

HAVE YOU SEEN HIM?

Someone should recognise the little guy. He's got 8 legs.

Teacher: *'What family does the octopus belong to?'*

Student: *'Nobody's I know.'*

Why can you believe everything a bearded teacher tells you?

They can't tell bare-faced lies.

Did you hear about the two history teachers who were dating?

They go to restaurants to talk about old times.

Why are maths teachers good at solving detective stories?

Because they know when all the clues add up.

What do you call a teacher with a school on his head?

Ed.

Teacher to parent: *'David's career choice as a train driver will suit him well. He has more experience of lines than any other student at this school!'*

First teacher: *'What's wrong with young Jimmy today? I saw him running around the playground, screaming and pulling at his hair.'*

Second teacher: *'Don't worry. He's just lost his marbles.'*

What word is always spelled wrong?
Wrong.

Maths teacher: *'Anne, why have you brought a picture of the queen of England with you today?'*

Anne: *'You told us to bring a ruler with us.'*

Student: *'I don't think I deserve a zero on this test.'*

Teacher: *'No, neither do I but it was the lowest I could give you!'*

Maths teacher: *'Richard, if you had 50 cents in each trouser pocket, and $2 in each blazer pocket, what would you have?'*

Richard: *'Someone else's uniform, Sir.'*

What kind of tests do witch teachers give?

Hex-aminations.

EEKK! That's definitely not a RABBIT SO I guess I failed the exam.

Teacher: *'Jessica, you aren't paying attention to me. Are you having trouble hearing?'*

Jessica: *'No, I'm having trouble listening.'*

Maths teacher: *'If you multiplied 1386 by 395, what would you get?'*

Student: *'The wrong answer.'*

Teacher: *'You missed school yesterday, didn't you?'*

Student: *'Not very much.'*

'Our teacher talks to herself in class, does yours?'

'Yes, but she doesn't realise it. She thinks we're listening!'

Playing truant from school is like having a credit card.

Lots of fun now, pay later.

Laugh, and the class laughs with you.

But you get detention alone.

Student: *'I didn't do my homework because I lost my memory.'*

Teacher: *'When did this start?'*

Student: *'When did what start?'*

Why was the head teacher worried?

Because there were so many rulers in the school.

Teacher: *'I told you to stand at the end of the line.'*

Student: *'I tried, but there was someone already there.'*

Miss! Miss! When Stuart shakes his head violently ... it RATTLES!!

RATTLE RATTLE RATTLE

Teacher: *'Why didn't you answer me, Stuart?'*

Stuart: *'I did, I shook my head.'*

Teacher: *'You don't expect me to hear it rattling from here, do you?'*

33

Teacher: '*I said to draw a cow eating grass, but you've only drawn a cow.*'

Student: '*Yes, the cow has eaten all the grass.*'

Did you hear about the teacher who locked the school band in a deep freeze?

They wanted to play really cool jazz.

Teacher: '*Why haven't you been to school for the last two weeks, Billy?*'

Billy: '*It's not my fault – whenever I go to cross the road outside, there's a man with a sign saying "Stop Children Crossing"!*'

Well... That's a great sign to have outside a school... I'm off home!

STOP CHILDREN CROSSING

Did you hear about the teacher who wore sunglasses to give out exam results?

He took a dim view of his students' performance.

History teacher: *'Why were ancient sailing ships so eco-friendly?'*

Student: *'Because they could go for hundreds of miles to the galleon.'*

How does a maths teacher know how long she sleeps?

She takes a ruler to bed.

Teacher: 'What's the name of a bird that doesn't build its own nest?'

Student: 'The cuckoo.'

Teacher: 'That's right – how did you know that?'

Student: 'Easy, Sir, everyone knows cuckoos live in clocks!'

Did you hear about the technology teacher who left teaching to try to make something of himself?

Why did the boy throw his watch out of the window during an exam?

Because he wanted to make time fly.

English teacher: *'James, give me a sentence with the word "counterfeit" in it.'*

James: *'I wasn't sure if she was a centipede or a millipede, so I had to count her feet.'*

Computer teacher: *'Sarah, give me an example of software.'*

Sarah: *'A floppy hat.'*

Student 1: *'We bought our retiring science teacher a gift – toilet water that cost $20.'*

Student 2: *'What! I would've sold you water from our toilets for only $2!'*

'What were you before you came to school, girls and boys?' asked the teacher, hoping that someone would say 'babies'. She was disappointed when all the children cried out, 'Happy!'

Before I came to school this morning... I was a tadpole.

Teacher: 'That's the stupidest boy in the whole school.'

Mother: 'That's my son.'

Teacher: 'Oh! I'm so sorry.'

Mother: 'You're sorry!'

'I hope you're not one of those boys who sits and watches the school clock,' said the principal to the new boy.

'No, Sir,' he replied. 'I've got a digital watch that beeps at three-fifteen!'

A new watch sonny?

IT'S 3.15 PM TELL THE PRINCIPAL IT'S TIME TO GO HOME

Teacher: 'Your daughter's only five and she can spell her name backwards? Why, that's remarkable!'

Mother: 'Yes, we're very proud of her.'

Teacher: 'And what is your daughter's name?'

Mother: 'Anna.'

My teacher says I've got such bad handwriting that I ought to be a doctor!

'**H**ow old would you say I am, Francis?' the teacher asked.

'Forty,' said the boy promptly.

'What makes you think I'm forty?' asked the puzzled teacher.

'My big brother is twenty,' he replied, 'and you're twice as silly as he is!'

'**D**o you like your new school, Billy?' asked Uncle Ned.

'Sometimes,' said the boy.

'When is that?'

'When it's closed!'

Ben's teacher thinks Ben is a wonder child.

She wonders whether he'll ever learn anything.

Simple Simon was writing a geography essay for his teacher. It began like this: *The people who live in Paris are called parasites.*

'*I'm not going to school today,*' said Alexander to his mother. '*The teachers bully me and the boys in my class don't like me. Why?*'

'*Firstly, you're 35 years old,*' replied his mother, '*and secondly, you're the principal!*'

'Be sure to go straight home from school.'

'I can't – I live around the corner!'

Teacher: 'Are you good at arithmetic?'

Mary: 'Well, yes and no.'

Teacher: 'What do you mean, yes and no?'

Mary: 'Yes, I'm no good at arithmetic.'

Teacher: 'If you had one dollar and asked your dad for one dollar, how much money would you have?'

Student: 'One dollar.'

Teacher: 'You don't know your maths.'

Student: 'You don't know my dad!'

There! There's a dollar for me... and another dollar for me... Now don't say I never give you anything!

Animal Crackers

MUM!
Has the elephant
been in my
bedroom again?

What time is it
when an elephant
climbs into your
bed?

*Time to get a new
bed.*

What do you get if you pour hot
water down a rabbit hole?

Hot cross bunnies.

Why do buffaloes always travel in herds?

Because they're afraid of getting mugged by elephants.

Why do elephants have trunks?

Because they can't fit everything into a handbag.

Where do elephants go on holidays?

Tuscany.

Why are elephants big and grey?
Because if they were small and purple they would be grapes.

What do you call the red stuff between an elephant's toes?
A slow explorer.

WOOPS...YUK! Looks like I've trod in another explorer!

Didn't see you there little guy!

Why do elephants have Big Ears?
Because Noddy wouldn't pay the ransom.

What do you call an amorous insect?
The love bug!

Where would
you find a dog
with no legs?

*Exactly where you
left it.*

What did the buffalo say to his son,
when he went away on a long trip?

'Bison.'

'Does your dog
bite?'

'No.'

'Oww. I thought
you said your dog
doesn't bite.'

'That's not my dog.'

46

Name an animal that lives in Lapland.

A reindeer.

Now name another.

Another reindeer.

What sits in the middle of the World Wide Web?

A very, very big spider.

Did you hear about the duck who bought some lipstick?

She asked the chemist to put it on her bill.

Did you hear about the acrobatic snake?

He was in Monty Python's Flying Circus.

Cow 1: 'Are you concerned about catching mad cow disease?'

Cow 2: 'Not at all. I'm a sheep.'

How did the frog die?

It Kermit-ted suicide.

Do you know where to find elephants?

Elephants don't need finding – they're so big they don't get lost.

What is a polygon?

A dead parrot.

Did you hear about the cannibal lioness?

She swallowed her pride.

What's the difference between a mouse and an elephant?

About a tonne.

What did the lioness say to the cub chasing the hunter?

Stop playing with your food.

What do you get when you cross a master criminal with a fish?

The Codfather.

49

What do you get when you cross a baby rabbit with a vegetable?

A bunion.

A grizzly bear walks into a bar and says to the bartender, 'I'll have a gin and . . . tonic.'

Bartender: *'What's with the big pause?'*

Bear: *'I don't know. My father had them, too.'*

My mother used to tell me my father was a grizzly bear on account of my big paws... But I won't believe a word of it!

Now do I look like a bear to you?

Why did the man cross a chicken with an octopus?

So everyone in his family could have a leg each.

How do you know when it's raining cats and dogs?

You step into a poodle.

How do pigs get clean?

They go to the hogwash.

What do you call it when a chimpanzee sprains his ankle?

A monkey wrench.

Why did the dinosaur cross the road?

Because there were no chickens.

I don't know why everyone's so keen to cross the road... There's nothing over here.

Where does a dinosaur cross a busy 6 Lane motorway? Anywhere it likes!!

What is white, lives in the Himalayas and lays eggs?

The Abominable Snow Chicken.

What happened to two frogs that caught the same bug at the same time?

They got tongue-tied.

What do you call a crazy chicken?

A cuckoo cluck.

What do you get if you cross Bambi with a ghost?

Bamboo.

How do cows count?

They use a cowculator.

7 cows plus 2 cows minus 3.5 cows equals..... Oh Moo! I'll need my cowculator for this one!

Why did the dinosaur not cross the road?

It was extinct.

How do you know when there is an elephant in the fridge?

There are footprints in the butter.

What's grey and can't see well from either end?

A donkey with its eyes shut.

Why are old dinosaur bones kept in a museum?

Because they can't find any new ones.

What's got six legs and can fly long distances?

Three swallows.

What do you get if you cross a pig with a zebra?

Striped sausages.

Now... if the striped sausages are ZEBRA... then the spotted ones must be LEOPARD. So then... what are the plain ones?

Did you hear about the monkey who left bits of his lunch all over the computer?

His dad went bananas.

What do you get if you cross a dinosaur with a werewolf?

Who knows, but I wouldn't want to be within a thousand miles of it when the moon is full!

Why did the cat sit on the computer?

To keep an eye on the mouse.

When do kangaroos celebrate their birthdays?

During leap years.

What do baby swans dance to?

Cygnet-ure tunes.

What is a duck's favourite TV show?

The feather forecast.

What did the rabbit give his girlfriend when they got engaged?

A 24-carrot ring.

Why don't baby birds smile?

Would you smile if your mother fed you worms all day?

What do you call a chicken that lays light bulbs?

A battery hen.

Why do bears have fur coats?

Because they can't get plastic raincoats in their size!

Where is the hottest place in the jungle?

Under a gorilla.

I don't know about you... but I'm finding it quite warm under here

Oh... so am I !

What would you get if you crossed a hunting dog with a journalist?

A news hound.

What do you get if you cross a parrot with a shark?

A bird that will talk your ear off!

Which birds steal the soap from the bath?

Robber ducks.

What do you get if you cross an electric eel with a sponge?

Shock absorbers.

Doctor, Doctor, I feel like a sheep.

That's baaaaaaaaaaad!

How do we know that owls are smarter than chickens?

Have you ever heard of Kentucky-fried owl?

When is a lion not a lion?

When he turns into his den.

Doctor, Doctor, I think I'm a python.

You can't get round me just like that, you know!

What does an octopus wear when it's cold?

A coat of arms.

WASH DAY AT THE OCTOPUS' PLACE

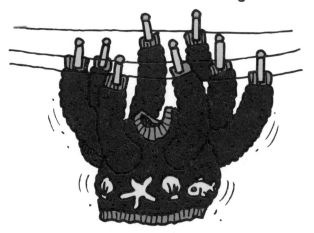

What's slimy, tastes of raspberry, is wobbly and lives in the sea?

A red jellyfish.

How do you know when a spider is cool?

It has its own website.

Now you see it, now you don't. What could you be looking at?

A black cat walking over a zebra crossing!

What did the mouse say to the elephant?

Squeak.

What's the difference between a dark sky and an injured lion?

One pours with rain, the other roars with pain.

What did the croaking frog say to her friend?

I think I've got a person in my throat.

What did the termite say when she saw that her friends had completely eaten a chair?

'Wooden you know it!'

Your chair was delicious... Do you mind if I try the table?

Sheep 1: *'Baa.'*

Sheep 2: *'I knew you were going to say that.'*

What are teenage giraffes told when they go on their first date?

No necking.

What did the boa constrictor say to its victim?

'I've got a crush on you.'

What disease do you have if you're allergic to horses?

Bronco-itis.

What do cats eat as a special treat?

Mice creams.

What do bees do with their honey?

They cell it.

What do bees use to communicate with each other?

Their cell phones.

How would you feel if you saw a
dinosaur in your backyard?

Very old.

When did the last dinosaur die?

After the second-last dinosaur.

What do you cut a dinosaur bone with?

A dino-saw.

What do you get when you cross a dinosaur with a pig?

Jurassic Pork.

What do cows listen to?

Moosic.

What groovy MOOSIC! I could moo along to this all day!

MOO MOO MOO

What do you call a baby whale that never stops crying?

A little blubber.

What do you call a camel with no humps?

A horse.

Why do elephants never get rich?

Because they work for peanuts.

What did the 100 kilo parrot say?

'Polly want a cracker, NOW!'

Did you hear about the duck decorator?

He papered over the quacks.

What did one bee say to her nosy neighbour bee?

'Mind your own bees' nest!'

What do you do with a mouse that squeaks?

You oil him.

How does a jellyfish race start?

Get set.

What do you call a cat who lives in a hospital?

A first aid kit.

What do you call a Chinese cat that spies through windows?

A Peking Tom.

What do you get when you cross a bear with a cow?

Winnie the Moo.

Gee! Thanks! What is it? Do I cuddle it... or do I milk it?

What do you get when you cross a black bird with a madman?

A raven lunatic.

What do you get when you cross a chicken with a cement mixer?

A bricklayer.

What do you get when you cross a cow with a clairvoyant?

A message from the udder side.

What do you get when you cross a shark with a crocodile and a Tyrannosauraus rex?

I don't know, but don't take it swimming.

What do you get when you cross
a cow with a whale?

Mooby Dick.

What do
you get if
you cross a
duck with a
firework?

A fire-quacker.

What do
you get when you
cross a hare with a walking stick?

A hurry-cane (hurricane).

What do you get when you cross
a kangaroo with a skyscraper?

A high jumper.

What do you get when you cross
a mouse and a deer?

Mickey Moose.

What do you get when you cross a
hippopotamus with someone who is
always sick?

A hippochondriac.

What do you get when you cross
a seagull with a pair of wheels?

A bi-seagull.

What do you get when you cross
a sheep with a radiator?

Central bleating.

What do you get when you cross
an elephant with a bottle of rum?

Trunk and disorderly.

What do you get
when you cross an
elephant with a
cake?

Crumbs.

Someone suggested a game of
'HERE COMES THE LION' at Jumbo's
3rd birthday party startling
his 2 ton friends into a stampede.

What language do birds speak?

Pigeon English.

What's as large as a horse but doesn't weigh anything?

Its shadow.

How do dinosaurs pay their bills?

With Tyrannosaurus cheques.

What do you get when you cross a Stegosaurus with a pig?

A porky spine.

How do dinosaurs pass exams?

With extinction.

What do you get when you cross a dinosaur with explosives?

Dino-mite.

What's the hardest part of making dinosaur stew?

Finding a pot big enough to hold the dinosaur.

What's the scariest dinosaur of all?

The Terrordactyl.

SCARY HEY?

The scariest thing in Prehistoric skies...
The Terrorsaurus

Where do dinosaurs go to the toilet?

In the dino-sewer.

Which dinosaur does well in English exams?

Tyrannathesaurus rex.

How did Noah steer the Ark at night?

He switched on the floodlights.

Why did the zookeeper refuse to work in the elephant enclosure?

Because the work kept piling up.

Why do chickens watch TV?

For hentertainment.

Why do frogs like beer?

Because it is made from hops.

What did Noah say as he was loading the animals?

'Now I herd everything.'

Why don't cats shave?

Because they prefer Whiskas.

WOH! Miss a day shaving and look what happens to those whiskers!

Why is the letter 'T' important to a stick insect?

Because without it, it would be a sick insect.

Why should you never fight an echidna?

Because she will always win on points.

Why was
the alligator
called
Kodak?

*Because he
was always
snapping.*

Just smile
and say...
CROCODILE!

Sorry....
ALLIGATOR!

Why did
the chicken
cross the
road, roll in
the mud and
cross the road again?

Because it was a dirty double-crosser.

Why did the chicken join the band?

Because it had drumsticks.

Why did the fish cross the sea?

To get to the other tide.

Why was the kangaroo mad at her children?

Because they were jumping on the bed.

Why was the little bear spoilt?

Because he was panda'd to.

Why wasn't the butterfly invited to the dance?

Because it was a moth ball.

81

Why are dolphins clever?

Because they live in schools.

Why can't frogs get life insurance?

Because they are always croaking.

Why can't you have a conversation with a goat?

Because it always butts in.

Which movie character do insects
like best?

Bug Lightyear.

Why are beavers so smart?

Because they gnaw everything.

Who is
the most
feared
animal
of all?

*Attila the
Hen.*

I never thought
that little chick
Attila would
turn out to be
such a wildgirl!

Which TV show do cows never miss?

The moos.

Which TV show do horses like best?

Neigh-bours.

Who is emperor of all mice?

Julius Cheeser.

Who is the king of the monkeys?

Henry the Ape.

Gold...
coins...
taxes...
wives...
Who needs them
Just bring me
BANANAS!

Why can't you play a practical joke on snakes?

Because they don't have a leg to pull.

Where would you weigh a whale?

At a whale-weigh station.

Which animals are best at maths?

Rabbits, because they're always multiplying.

YAKKITY YAK...YAKKITY YAKKITTY YAKKITY YAKKITY YAK... Did you hear the joke about the yak that couldn't stop YAKKING?

YAKK YAKK

Which animal never stops talking?

The yak.

Why YAKS are found only in the highest mountains of the Himalayas!

Which bird can lift the heaviest weights?

The crane.

85

Which bird never grows up?

The minor bird.

Which bird succeeds?

A budgie without teeth.

Which hen lays the longest?

A dead one.

Which area of the police force accepts monkeys?

The Special Branch.

What's the difference between a bird and a fly?

A bird can fly but a fly can't bird.

What's the difference between a buffalo and a bison?

You can't wash your hands in a buffalo.

What's the healthiest insect?

A vitamin bee.

With this new Vitamin BEE I feel all ... ... A-BUZZ

BUZZ BUZZ BUZZ BUZZ

VITAMIN BEE

When is a brown dog not a brown dog?

When it's a greyhound.

When is
the best
time to buy
a canary?

*When it's
going cheap.*

Where did the cow go for its holiday?

Moo Zealand.

Where do baby
elephants come
from?

Very big storks.

Where do baby monkeys sleep?

In an apricot.

Where do chickens go to die?

To oven.

Where did
Noah keep the
bees?

In the ark hives.

39 days ago
we only had
2 of these
bees when
we boarded
the Ark...
Now we're
swarming in
them!

Where do
cows go for
entertainment?

The moovies.

Where do monkeys cook
their dinner?

Under the gorilla.

89

Food for Thought

What can you serve, but never eat?
A tennis ball.

What vegetable
goes well with jacket
potatoes?
Button mushrooms.

What jam can't you eat?

A traffic jam!

What is a goalkeeper's favourite snack?

Beans on post!

What do you get when you cross an orange with a squash court?

Orange squash.

What happened when there was a fight in the fish and chip shop?

Two fish got battered.

What's the difference between a young lady and a fresh loaf?

One is a well-bred maid and the other is well-made bread.

What did one tomato say to the other that was lagging behind?

Ketchup!

Where all the slow tomatoes end up.

What is the difference between a hungry person and a greedy person?

One longs to eat, and the other eats too long.

What do termites eat for dessert?

Toothpicks.

What's green and short and goes camping?

A boy sprout.

What's the difference between a nightwatchman and a butcher?

One stays awake and the other weighs a steak!

Why did the farmer plough his field with a steamroller?

He wanted to grow mashed potatoes.

What do you get if you cross Frankenstein with a hot dog?

Frankenfurterstein.

What should you take if a monster invites you to dinner?

Someone who can't run as fast as you.

What did the dragon say when he saw St George in his shining armour?

'Oh no! Not more tinned food!'

94

When the cannibal crossed the Pacific
on a cruise ship, he told the waiter
to take the menu away and bring
him the passenger list!

Where do ants eat?

A restaur-ant.

What do you do if your chicken
feels sick?

Give her an eggs-ray.

Why did the monster eat the
light bulb?

He wanted some light refreshment.

Mother: *'I told you not to eat cake before supper.'*

Son: *'But it's part of my homework – see – if you take an eighth of a cake from a whole cake, how much is left?'*

Lucy: *'If you eat any more ice cream, you'll burst.'*

Lindy: *'Okay – pass the ice cream and duck.'*

What does a Yeti eat for dinner?

An ice-burger.

Knock knock.

Who's there?

Bach!

Bach who?

Bach of chips!

Knock knock.

Who's there?

Bacon!

Bacon who?

Bacon a cake for your birthday!

A man went into a cafe and ordered two slices of apple pie with four scoops of ice cream, covered with lashings of raspberry sauce and piles of chopped nuts.

'Would you like a cherry on top?' asked the waitress.

'No thanks,' said the man. *'I'm on a diet.'*

97

What do vultures always have for dinner?

Leftovers.

How do you make a cream puff?

Make it run around the block.

What is a termite's favourite breakfast?

Oak-meal.

Why did the lazy boy get a job in a bakery?

Because he wanted a good loaf!

Knock knock.

Who's there?

Beef!

Beef who?

Bee fair now!

Doctor, Doctor, I keep getting a pain in the eye when I drink coffee.

Have you tried taking the spoon out of the cup before you drink?

Well... if COFFEE affects you like that ...give it up!

Knock knock.

Who's there?

Brie!

Brie who?

Brie me my supper!

99

Knock knock.
Who's there?
Butcher!
Butcher who?
Butcher arms around me!

Have you ever seen a man-eating tiger?
No, but in a restaurant next door I once saw a man eating chicken . . .

Waiter, I can't eat this meal. Fetch me the manager.
It's no use. He won't eat it either.

Waiter, how did this fly get in my soup?

I guess it flew.

Waiter, do you have frogs' legs?

Yes sir.

Then hop to the kitchen and fetch me a steak.

When the wally's co-worker asked why he had a sausage stuck behind his ear, he replied, '*Oh – I must have eaten my pencil for lunch!*'

Gee...I'm glad I always carry a spare sausage behind my ear to write with.

How do you make a banana split?
Cut it in half.

How do you make a French fry?
Leave him in the sun.

How do you make a fruit punch?
Give it boxing lessons.

'**Y**our finger is in my bowl of soup!' said the man.

'Don't worry,' said the wally waiter. 'The soup isn't hot.'

My left thumb thinks it's Cream of Chicken ...my right thinks it's Pumpkin!

What happened to the male bee who fell in love?

He got stuck on his honey.

What's the best way to face a timid mouse?

Lie down in front of its mouse hole and cover your nose with cheese spread!

Where do sharks shop?

The fish market.

What do fishermen eat at Easter?

Oyster eggs.

What's a lawyer's favourite dessert?

Suet.

What's rhubarb?

Embarrassed celery.

Doctor, Doctor, should I surf the Internet on an empty stomach?

No, you should do it on a computer.

How do you start a race between two rice puddings?

Sago.

What did the mayonnaise say to the fridge?

'Close the door, I'm dressing.'

Doctor, Doctor, I feel like an apple.

We must get to the core of this!

'William,' shouted his mum. *'There were two pieces of cake in that pantry last night, and now there's only one. How do you explain that?'*

'It was dark in the pantry,' said William. *'And I didn't see the second piece!'*

LOOK...! NO CAKE!

Waiter, there's a fly in my soup.

Well you did order fly soup, ma'am.

Waiter, what kind
of soup is this?

Bean soup.

I don't care
what it's been.
What is it
now?

Is it any wonder I'm a SOURPUSS...
That's not lemonade!
That's VINEGAR!

Charley: *'My
cat likes to
drink lemonade.'*

Lenny: *'Golly,
he sure must be
a sourpuss!'*

Dick and Jane were arguing over the breakfast table.

'Oh, you're so stupid!' shouted Dick.

'Dick!' said their father. 'That's quite enough! Now say you're sorry.'

'Okay,' said Dick. 'Jane, I'm sorry you're stupid.'

Johnny collected lots of money from trick-or-treating and he went to the store to buy some chocolate.

'You should give that money to charity,' said the shopkeeper.

'No thanks,' replied Johnny. 'I'll buy the chocolate – you give the money to charity!'

What kind of
sharks never eat
women?

Man-eating sharks.

How do you make a swiss roll?

Push him down a hill.

How do you make an apple crumble?

Smash it with a mallet.

Two cannibals
were having lunch.

*'Your girlfriend
makes a great soup,'*
said one to the
other.

'Yes!' agreed the
first. *'But I'm going to miss her!'*

How do you make an egg laugh?

Tell it a yolk.

Why did the girl feed money to her cow?

Because she wanted to get rich milk.

Why did the girl put a chicken in
a tub of hot water?

*Because she wanted the chicken to lay
hard-boiled eggs!*

'It's a pity you've gone on
a hunger strike,' said the
convict's girlfriend on
visiting day.

'Why?' asked the convict.

'Because I've put a file in
your cake!'

Oh come on...
I can handle
a hair...or even
half a cockroach
in a cake...
but not a FILE!

Girl: *'How much is a soft drink?'*

Waitress: *'Fifty cents.'*

Girl: *'How much is a refill?'*

Waitress: *'The first is free.'*

Girl: *'Well then, I'll have a refill.'*

Knock knock.

Who's there?

Cantaloupe!

Cantaloupe who?

Cantaloupe with you tonight!

What do you call an egg in the jungle?

An eggsplorer.

Knock knock.

Who's there?

Zubin!

Zubin who?

Zubin eating garlic again!

Amy: *'Did you find your cat?'*

Karen: *'Yes, he was in the refrigerator.'*

Amy: *'Goodness, is he okay?'*

Karen: *'He's more than okay – he's a cool cat!'*

Waiter, I'd like burnt steak and soggy chips with a grimy, bitter salad.

I'm afraid the chef won't cook that for you, sir.

Why not? He did yesterday.

Which cheese is made backwards?

Edam.

What vegetable can you play snooker with?

A cue-cumber.

What's the difference between school lunches and a pile of slugs?

School lunches are on plates.

The cruise-ship passenger was feeling really seasick, when the waiter asked if he'd like some lunch.

'No thanks,' he replied. 'Just throw it over the side and save me the trouble.'

What's small, round, white and giggles?

A tickled onion.

What do nudists like to eat best?

Skinless sausages.

What do lions say before they go out hunting for food?

Let us prey.

Why did the tomato blush?

Because it saw the salad dressing.

What's a lion's favourite food?

Baked beings.

Why do gingerbread men wear trousers?

Because they have crummy legs.

A mushroom walks into a bar and says to the bartender, *'Get me a drink!'*

We don't serve fungus at this bar! Besides... you're dropping spores all over the counter!

But the bartender refuses.

The mushroom says, *'Why not? I'm a fun-gi!'*

Why do watermelons get married?

Because they can't-elope.

Why does steak taste better in space?

Because it is meteor.

Why don't nuts
go out at night?

*Because they don't
want to be assaulted.*

What do you get
when you cross an
overheating Apple
computer with fast food?

A Big Mac and fries.

Waiter,
there's a
cockroach
in my soup.

*Sorry sir,
we're all out
of flies.*

What are monsters' favourite lunches?

Shepherd's pie and ploughman's lunch.

How does Frankenstein eat?

He bolts his food down.

Knock knock.

Who's there?

U-8!

U-8 who?

U-8 my lunch!

True

Colours

What's green,
covered in
custard and
sad?

Apple grumble.

What's red on
the outside and
green inside?

A dinosaur wearing red pyjamas.

118

Boy monster: 'You've got a face like a million dollars.'

Girl monster: 'Have I really?'

Boy monster: 'Sure, it's green and wrinkly!'

Boy: 'Dad there's a black cat in the dining room!'

Dad: 'That's okay son, black cats are lucky.'

Son: 'This one is – he's eaten your dinner!'

What do you do with a blue monster?

Try to cheer him up a bit.

Three girls walked into a barber shop. Two had blonde hair and one had green hair. The barber asked the blondes, *'How did you get to be blonde?'*

You know... you can get the same look just by using green mousse.

'Oh, it's natural,' they replied.

The barber asked the other girl, *'How did your hair become green?'*

She replied – (now put your hand on your nose and rub up to your hair . . .)

What is red, sweet and bites people?

A jampire!

Why do we dress baby girls in pink and baby boys in blue?

Because babies can't dress themselves.

Obviously radical babies

Visitor: *'You're very quiet, Louise.'*

Louise: *'Well, my mum gave me a dollar not to say anything about your red nose.'*

If everyone bought a white car, what would we have?

A white carnation.

'Is that the computer help line? Every time I log on to the Seven Dwarves website, my computer screen goes snow white . . .'

What do you get if you cross a teacher and a traffic warden?

Someone who gives you 500 double yellow lines for being late.

What's the tallest yellow flower in the world?

A giraffodil.

Why did the monster paint himself in rainbow coloured stripes?

He wanted to hide in a pencil case.

What's black and white and red all over?

A sunburned zebra.

I figure that zebras only get half sunburnt... We only get red on the white parts!

What's green and hard?

A frog that lifts weights.

What's red and white?

Pink.

Who steals from her grandma's house?

Little Red Robin Hood.

What colour is a hiccup?

Burple.

What's red, white and brown and travels faster than the speed of sound?

An astronaut's ham and tomato sandwich.

What's green and pecks on trees?

Woody Wood Pickle.

What's green, has two legs and sits on the end of your finger?

The boogieman.

What's green and sings?

Elvis Parsley.

What's green and slimy and hangs from trees?

Giraffe boogie.

What's yellow and square?

A tomato in disguise.

Knock knock.

Who's there?

Beezer.

Beezer who?

Beezer black and yellow
and make honey.

What goes in pink
and comes out blue?

*A swimmer on a
cold day!*

What's black and white and rolls
down a hill?

A penguin.

What's black and white and laughs?

The penguin who pushed the other one.

What's big and white and can't jump over a fence?

A fridge.

Which king was purple and had many wives?

King Henry the Grape.

What's grey, has four legs and a trunk?

A mouse going on holiday.

Whatever possessed me to drag a heavy trunk around the world? I should have settled for a soft vinyl overnight bag with a zipper!

What's purple, 5000 years old and 400 kilometres long?

The Grape Wall of China.

What's thick and black and picks its nose?

Crude oil.

How many clothing shop assistants does it take to change a light bulb?

Three, one to change it, one to say how well it fits and one to say that the colour is perfect.

Rude and Crude

You're such a bad cook, even the maggots get takeaway.

Your family is so weird, when the doorbell rings your sister has to shout out 'Ding, dong.'

You are as useless as a screen door on a submarine.

With you here, your village must be missing its idiot.

Don't let your mind wander – it's too little to be let out alone.

Statistics say that one in three people is wacky.

So check your friends and if two of them seem okay, you're the one . . .

Here's 50 cents. Call all your friends and bring me back the change.

Your dog is so slow, he brings in last week's newspaper.

Turn the other cheek. On second thoughts, don't. The view is just as ugly on that side.

O.K.! Give me your best side!

This is my best side!

Oh Brother!

You're not as stupid as you look. That would be impossible.

I'd leave you with one thought if you had somewhere to put it.

Your feet are so smelly, your shoes refuse to come out of the closet.

The other shoes in the wardrobe could stand the smell no longer... so the stinky sandshoes were shown the door...

If it's true that opposites attract, you'll meet someone who is good-looking, intelligent and cultured.

Everyone has the right to be ugly, but you abused the privilege.

She's so ugly, when a wasp stings her, it has to shut its eyes!

If someone offered you a penny for your thoughts, they'd expect some change.

You're dark and handsome. When it's dark, you're handsome.

Last time I saw someone as ugly as you, I had to pay admission.

As an outsider, what do you think of the human race?

Instead of drinking from the fountain of knowledge, you just gargled.

They say that truth is stranger than fiction. And you're the proof.

I'll never forget the first time we met – although I keep trying.

Someone told me you're not fit to live with pigs but I stuck up for you and said you were.

You're so boring, you won't even talk to yourself.

You're so ugly, the only dates you get are on a calendar.

135

You're so ugly you have to trick or treat over the phone.

You're growing on me – like a wart.

'Daddy, can I have another glass of water, please?'

'Okay, but that's the twelfth one I've given you tonight.'

'Yes I know, but the house is still on fire.'

'Can I go swimming now, Mum?'
asked the child.

'No – there are sharks at this beach,'
said his mother.

'Dad's swimming!'

Yes, he's got a million dollars' life
insurance . . .'

George is the
type of boy that
his mother doesn't
want him to hang
around with . . .

Are you all nice and tidy to go out George? Have you got a clean hanky and underpants?

Did you hear
about the two fat
men who ran a
marathon?

One ran in short bursts, the other
ran in burst shorts.

A woman woke her husband in the middle of the night.

'There's a burglar in the kitchen eating the cake I made this morning!' she said.

'Who should I call?' asked her husband. *'The police or an ambulance?'*

My cousin spent heaps on deodorant, until he found out people just didn't like him ...

Did you hear about the two bodies cremated at the same time?

It was a dead heat.

Did you hear about the dentist who became a brain surgeon?

His drill slipped.

What's the difference between a peeping Tom and someone who's just got out of the bath?

One is rude and nosey. The other is nude and rosey!

There's no point in telling some people a joke with a double meaning.

They wouldn't understand either of them!

Three guys, Shutup, Manners and Poop, drove too fast and Poop fell out of the car.

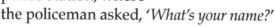

Shutup went to the police station, where the policeman asked, *'What's your name?'*

'Shutup,' he answered.

'Hey – where are your manners!' the policeman exclaimed.

Shutup replied, *'Outside on the road, scrapin' up Poop!'*

As he was walking along a street, the minister saw a little girl trying to reach a high door knocker. Anxious to help, he went over to her. *'Let me do it, dear,'* he said, rapping the knocker.

'Thanks,' said the little girl. *'Now run like heck!'*

Why did the female frog lay eggs?
Because her husband spawned her affections.

Uncle Herbert noticed that his nephew Johnny was watching him all the time.

'Why are you always looking at me?' he asked.

'I was just wondering when you were going to do your trick,' replied Johnny.

'What trick?' asked Uncle Herbert.

'Well, Mum says you eat like a horse . . .'

A man out for a walk came across a little boy pulling his cat's tail.

'Hey you!' he shouted. 'Don't pull the cat's tail!'

'I'm not pulling,' replied the boy. 'I'm only holding on – the cat's doing the pulling. . .'

My dad once stopped a man ill-treating a donkey.

It was a case of brotherly love. . .

What do you get when you cross a vampire with a dwarf?

A monster which sucks blood out of people's kneecaps.

142

When the man was run over by a steamroller, what was proved?

That he had lots of guts.

The next scene is just too ugly to draw...!

Why shouldn't you sleep on trains?

They run over sleepers!

What do you call a one-legged woman?

Eileen!

Roger was in a full bus when a fat lady opposite said to him, *'If you were a gentleman, you'd stand up and let someone else sit down.'*

'And if you were a lady,' Roger replied, *'you'd stand up and let four people sit down!'*

Now listen here sonny-Jim ... If you were any sort of gentleman you'd use that crow bar you've got there to lever me out of this seat!

A woman was facing court, charged with wounding her husband.

'You're very lucky you're not facing a murder charge – why did you stab him over a hundred times?' asked the judge.

'I didn't know how to turn off the electric carving knife,' she replied.

W hat is the smelliest game in the world?

Ping pong!

World of Sport

What has 75 pairs of sneakers, a ball and two hoops?

A centipede basketball team.

Where do footballers dance?

At a football!

Why didn't the wally goalkeeper catch the ball?

He thought that's what the net was for.

Hey... you'll have to do that again... I wasn't ready!

'I can't see us ever finishing this tenpin bowling game.'

'Why is that?'

'Every time I knock all the pins down, someone calls everyone out on strike!'

I don't know how many soccer players it takes to change a lightbulb... but whoever kicked the ball can change it.

How many soccer players does it take to change a light bulb?

Eleven, one to change it, the others to jump about, hugging and kissing him.

Why aren't football stadiums built in outer space?

Because there is no atmosphere!

Which goalkeeper can jump higher than a crossbar?

All of them – a crossbar can't jump!

What's a pig's favourite ballet?

Swine Lake.

What baseball position did the boy
with no arms or legs play?

Home base.

What job does
Dracula have with
the Transylvanian
baseball team?

*He looks after the
bats.*

What do you call a cat that plays
football?

Puss in boots.

What lights up a football stadium?

A football game!

W hy do football
coaches bring
suitcases along to
away games?

*So that they can
pack the defence!*

I f you have a
referee in football,
what do you have in bowls?

Cornflakes!

H ow do hens encourage their
football teams?

They egg them on!

H ow do you start a doll's race?

Ready, Teddy, Go!

Who won the race between two balls of string?

They were tied!

How did the basketball court get wet?

The players dribbled all over it!

Why don't grasshoppers go to football matches?

They prefer cricket matches!

151

Why didn't the dog want to play football?

It was a boxer!

When fish play football, who is the captain?

The team's kipper!

How do you stop squirrels playing football in the garden?

Hide the ball, it drives them nuts!

Why should you be careful when playing against a team of big cats?

They might be cheetahs!

YES! Here's the ball. I'm going for a goal!

Name a tennis player's favourite city.

Volley Wood!

Where do football directors go when they are sick of the game?

The bored room!

What's a vampire's favourite sport?

Batminton.

Why BATMINTON? Why couldn't he have taken up... mountain climbing or cake decorating?

What do vampire footballers have at half time?

Blood oranges.

Coach: 'I thought I told you to lose weight. What happened to your three-week diet?'

Player: 'I finished it in three days!'

What do you get when you cross a skunk with a table-tennis ball?

Ping pong.

How many baseball players does it take to change a light bulb?

Two, one to change it, the other to signal which way to do it.

What do you get
when you cross
a plumber with a
ballerina?

A tap dancer.

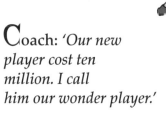

Coach: *'Our new
player cost ten
million. I call
him our wonder player.'*

Fan: *'Why's that?'*

Coach: *'Every time he plays, I wonder
why I bothered to buy him!'*

Coach: *'I'll give you $100 a week to start
with, and $500 a week in a year's time.'*

Young player: *'See you in a year!'*

What did the football player say when he accidentally burped during the game?

'Sorry, it was a freak hic!'

What part of a basketball stadium is never the same?

The changing rooms!

What happens when an athlete gets angry with his computer?

He becomes a floppy diskus thrower.

Where do old bowling balls end up?

In the gutter!

Why do artists never win when they play basketball?

They keep drawing!

What are Brazilian fanatics called?

Brazil nuts!

What did they call Dracula when he won the premiership?

The Champire!

Why does someone who runs marathons make a good student?

Because education pays off in the long run!

What stories are told by basketball players?

Tall stories!

Why did the golfer wear two pairs of trousers?

In case he got a hole in one.

When you've finished skipping... Can we get on with the game?

Why did the footballer take a piece of rope onto the pitch?

He was the skipper!

What wears nine gloves, 18 shoes and a mask?

A baseball team.

Why was the struggling manager seen shaking the club cat?

To see if there was any money in the kitty!

Music to My Ears

Why did the singer
climb a ladder?

To reach the high notes.

Did you hear about
the wally burglar?

*He robbed a music store
and stole the lute.*

160

How many country music singers does it take to change a light bulb?

Two, one to change it, the other to sing about how heartbroken he is that the old one is finished.

What type of music do mummies like best?

Ragtime.

Back in my day we used to dance to Ragtime. These days it's just all this RAP stuff!

What's a skeleton's favourite musical instrument?

A trom-bone.

'My brother's been practising the violin for ten years.'

Is he any good?

'No, it was nine years before he found out he wasn't supposed to blow!'

Knock knock.

Who's there?

Cecil.

Cecil who?

Cecil have music wherever she goes.

What do you call a guy who hangs around musicians?

A drummer.

What type of music do zombies like best?

Soul music.

You'd find dancing to this ROCK MUSIC would be much easier with this quartz. That granite is far too heavy!

What type of music do geologists like best?

Rock.

What sort of music is played most in the jungle?

Snake, rattle and roll.

Why did the monster eat his music teacher?

His Bach was worse than his bite.

What was Pavarotti before he was a tenor?

A niner.

What do you call a small Indian guitar?

A baby sitar.

Where do musicians live?

In A flat.

'This piece of music is haunting.'

That's because you're murdering it.

The painful murder of the "1812 overture"

How do you make a bandstand?

Take away their chairs.

'I played Beethoven last night.'

'Who won?'

I dig that groovy sole music!

Why did the footballer hold his boot to his ear?

Because he liked sole music!

165

'What shall I sing next?'

'Do you know "Bridge Over Troubled Waters?"'

'Yes.'

'Then go and jump off it.'

What do Eskimos sing at birthday parties?

'Freeze a Jolly Good Fellow.'

I wish someone would move me closer to the candles...so I could thaw out enough to blow them out!

What does a musician take to the supermarket?

A Chopin Lizst.

What instrument does a fisherman play?

A cast-a-net.

'Our Jackie learnt to play the violin in no time at all.'

'So I can hear.'

Why couldn't the composer be found?

Because he was Haydn.

Why was the musician in prison?

Because he was always getting into treble.

Where do musical frogs perform?

At the Hopera House.

What kind of song can you sing in the car?

A cartoon (car tune)!

Dumb and Dumber

You're so dumb, when you eat
M&Ms, you throw out the Ws.

You're so ugly, when you enter
a room, the mice jump on chairs.

You're so dumb, you took your mobile phone back to the shop because it came without a cord.

You're so dumb, it takes you an hour to cook one-minute noodles.

Did you hear what Dumb Donald did when he offered to paint the garage for his dad?

The instructions said put on three coats – so he put on his jacket, his raincoat and his overcoat!

170

My girlfriend talks so much that when she goes on vacation, she has to spread suntan lotion on her tongue!

Little Susie stood in the department store near the escalator, watching the moving handrail.

'Something wrong, little girl?' asked the security guard.

'Nope,' replied Susie. *'I'm just waiting for my chewing gum to come back.'*

Emma: *'What a cool pair of odd socks you have on, Jill.'*

Jill: *'Yes, and I have another pair just like it at home.'*

Oh... I can't wear these socks out tonight... They've got a hole in them!

Dad: *'Don't be selfish. Let your brother use the sled half the time.'*

Son: *'I do, Dad. I use it going down the hill and he gets to use it coming up the hill!'*

Why did the lion feel sick after he'd eaten the priest?

Because it's hard to keep a good man down.

You're so dumb, when you went to the mind reader they couldn't find anything to read.

In your mind young man... I see.... NOTHING! But for another $10 I'm sure I could find something.'

'**D**ad, can you write in the dark?'

'I suppose so.'

'Good. Can you sign my report card, please?'

'**M**um, I'm not going to school today.'

'Why not?'

'Because it's Sunday.'

My big brother is such an idiot. The other day I saw him hitting himself over the head with a hammer.

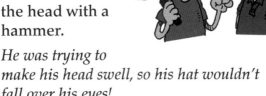

He was trying to make his head swell, so his hat wouldn't fall over his eyes!

Why did Silly Sue throw her guitar away?

Because it had a hole in the middle.

A man whose son had just passed his driving test came home one evening and found that the boy had driven into the living room.

'How did you manage that?' he fumed.

'Quite simple, Dad,' said the boy. *'I just came in through the kitchen and turned left.'*

'Why are you crying, Ted?' asked his mum.

'Because my new sneakers hurt,' Ted replied.

'That's because you've put them on the wrong feet.'

'But they're the only feet I have!'

174

'**M**um, Mum, Dad's broken my computer!'

'How did he do that?'

'I dropped it on his head!'

Did you hear about my brother?

He saw a moose's head hanging on a wall and went into the next room to find the rest of it!

A boy was staying in an old house, and in the middle of the night, he met a ghost.

'I've been walking these corridors for 300 years,' said the ghost.

'In that case, can you tell me where the bathroom is?' asked the boy.

First witch: *'I took my son to the zoo yesterday.'*

Second witch: *'Really? Did they keep him?'*

Did you hear about the farmer's boy who hated the country?

He went to the big city and got a job as a shoeshine boy, and so the farmer made hay while the sun shone.

Mum: *'How can you practise your trumpet and listen to the radio at the same time?'*

Son: *'Easy, I have two ears!'*

'**M**um,' Richard yelled from the kitchen. '*You know that dish you were always worried I'd break?*'

Mum won't be too mad.... It's only broken into 3 big bits.

'*Yes dear, what about it?*' said his mum.

'*Well . . . your worries are over.*'

'**M**um, *there's a man at the door collecting for the Old Folks' Home,*' said the little boy. '*Shall I give him Grandma?*'

Two girls were having lunch in the school yard. One had an apple, and the other said, '*Watch out for worms, won't you!*'

The first girl replied, '*Why should I? They can watch out for themselves!*'

What do you call a top girl-group made up of nits?

The Lice Girls!

Why did the boy wear a life jacket in bed?

Because he slept on a waterbed.

Jane: *'Do you like me?'*

Wayne: *'As girls go, you're fine . . . and the sooner you go, the better!'*

Dad was taking Danny around the museum, when they came across a magnificent stuffed lion in a case.

'Dad,' asked a puzzled Danny, *'how did they shoot the lion without breaking the glass?'*

Boy: *'Grandpa, do you know how to croak?'*

Why is it that everyone thinks old frogs are rolling in cash?

Is it because I'm about to CROAK?

Grandpa: *'No, I don't. Why?'*

Boy: *'Because Daddy says he'll be a rich man when you do!'*

You're so slow, you can't even catch your breath.

John: *'Have you noticed your mother smells a bit funny these days?'*

Will: *'No. Why?'*

John: *'Well, your sister told me she was giving her a bottle of toilet water for her birthday!'*

179

You're so dumb, when your teacher said she wanted you to get ahead, she really meant 'a head'.

'**M**um, can I please change my name right now?' asked Ben.

'Why would you want to do that, dear?' asked his mum.

'Because Dad says he's going to ground me, as sure as my name's Benjamin!'

What does a wally pour over his meat?

Thick gravy.

George knocked on the door of his friend's house. When his friend's mother answered he asked, *'Can Albert come out to play?'*

'No,' said Albert's mother. *'It's too cold.'*

'Well then,' said George, *'can his football come out to play?'*

'William, I've been told you tried to put paint on two boys at school,' said his dad.

'Yes Dad,' said William.

'They are twins and I needed a way to tell them apart!'

Did you hear about the girl who was so keen on road safety that she always wore white at night?

Last winter she was knocked down by a snow plough.

What do young female monsters do at parties?

They go around looking for edible bachelors!

One day Joe's mother said to his father, *'It's such a nice day, I think I'll take Joe to the zoo.'*

'I wouldn't bother,' said his father. *'If they want him, let them come and get him!'*

Why did the wally team always lose the tug of war?

They pushed . . .

Did you hear about the wally who went waterskiing?

He spent his whole holiday looking for a sloping lake.

Did you hear about the wally pirate?

He had a patch over both eyes.

183

Did you hear about the wally school kid who was studying Greek mythology?

When the teacher asked him to name something that was half-man and half-beast he replied, 'Buffalo Bill'.

Handsome Harry: *'Every time I walk past a girl, she sighs.'*

Wisecracking William: *'With relief!'*

Ahhr... MR Mummy... SIR.. would it be OK to take your daughter on a date ...cruise the Nile... see some Pyramids?

Why was the Egyptian girl worried?

Because her Daddy was a Mummy!

Heard about the foolish karate champion who joined the army?

The first time he saluted, he nearly killed himself.

ATTENN-SHUNNN!

WAK!

The teacher told Wally he knew he'd skipped school last Friday, and heard he'd been playing at the games arcade.

Wally told him it wasn't true – and he had the football game tickets to prove it!

Robert was a wally – he saw a sign outside a police station that read: 'Man Wanted For Robbery,' so he went in and applied for the job!

Why did the wally get 17 of his friends to accompany him to the movies?

Because he'd heard it was not for under-18s.

The gangland boss was surprised to find one of his gang sawing the legs off his bed.

'Why are you doing that?' he asked.

'Well, you did ask me to lie low for a bit,' the wally replied.

Susie asked the wally if his tent leaked when he was on holiday.

'Only when it rained,' he said.

'Are you lost?' the policeman asked the wally schoolgirl.

'Of course not,' she replied. 'I'm here, it's my school that's lost.'

Why did the wally pilot land his plane on a house?

Because they'd left the landing lights on.

Did you hear about the wally hitchhiker?

He got up early so there wouldn't be much traffic around.

Have you heard about the wally who went into an 'Open 24 hours a day' store and asked what time they closed?

'Do you turn on your computer with your left hand or your right hand?'

'My right hand.'

'Amazing! Most people have to use the on/off switch!'

OK... This must be a trick question. That's my LEFT HAND... That's my RIGHT HAND... So where's the ON/OFF SWITCH?

Customer: 'I cleaned my computer and now it doesn't work.'

Repairman: 'What did you clean it with?'

Customer: 'Soap and water.'

Repairman: 'Water's never meant to get near a computer!'

Customer: 'Oh, I bet it wasn't the water that caused the problem . . . it was when I put it in the spin dryer!'

How do you milk a mouse?

You can't. The bucket won't fit under it.

How do you stop a dog doing his business in the hall?

Put him outside.

'**I** play Scrabble with my pet dog every night.'

'He must be clever.'

'I don't know about that. I usually beat him.'

'I've lost my dog.'

'Put an ad in the paper.'

'Don't be silly. He can't read.'

What do you get when you cross a flower with a wally?

A blooming idiot.

eeee...hee..hee... ooh...ooh...ahhrr

GREAT! A plant with a mental problem!

A wally went to the train station.

Wally: *'I'd like a return ticket please.'*

Ticket seller: *'Certainly sir, where to?'*

'Back here of course.'

How many wallies does it take to change a light bulb?

Five, one to climb the ladder, the others to turn the ladder around and around.

'Wally, what's the weather like?'

'I don't know. It's too foggy to tell.'

WOH! Is it just me... or is it foggy today?

A wally was just about to dive into a pool when a lifesaver came rushing up.

Lifesaver: *'Don't jump. There's no water in the pool.'*

Wally: *'It's okay. I can't swim.'*

D id you hear about the wally glass blower?

He inhaled and got a pane in the tummy.

Did you hear about the wally secretary?

She was so good she could type 60 mistakes a minute.

Did you hear about the wally shoe repairman?

A customer gave him a pair of shoes to be soled, so he sold them.

Did you hear about the wally who had a brain transplant?

The brain rejected him.

I feel rejected. Even my brain has left me!

I'm outa here!

Did you hear about the wally shoplifter?

He hurt his back trying to lift the corner store.

Did you hear about the other wally shoplifter?

He stole a free sample.

Did you hear about the wally photographer?

He saved used light bulbs for his dark room.

Why did the wally throw away
his doughnut?

Because it had a hole in the middle.

Did you hear about the wally who
locked his keys in the car?

*He called a mechanic to get his
family out.*

Did you hear about the wally water
polo player?

His horse drowned.

Did you hear about the wally who spent two hours in a department store?

Boy! These caps with a peak at the back are hard to come by! But at last I found one.

He was looking for a cap with a peak at the back.

Did you hear about the wally who stole a calendar?

He got 12 months.

Did you hear about the wally glazier who tried to fit a new window?

He broke it with a hammer.

What did the
wally window
cleaner have on
the top of his
ladder?

A stop sign.

Did you hear
about the wally
who wanted
value for money?

*He sat at the back of the bus
to get a longer ride.*

Did you hear about the wally who
went skiing?

*He skied up the slope and caught the chair
lift down.*

How did the wally burn his ear?

He was ironing when the phone rang.

What about the wally who burnt both his ears?

The caller rang back.

Why did the dinosaur fall out of a palm tree?

Because a hippopotamus pushed him out.

Why do dinosaurs wear glasses?

So they don't step on other dinosaurs.

Did you hear about the boy who wanted to run away to the circus?

He ended up in a flea circus!

'**W**hat's the difference between a marshmallow and a pykost?'

'What's a pykost?'

'About two dollars.'

'**M**ay I try on that dress in the window?'

'No. I'm afraid you'll have to use the dressing room like everyone else.'

Love Me Tender

What happened when the young wizard met the young witch?

It was love at first fright.

Why is a bride always out of luck on her wedding day?

Because she never marries the best man.

What did the undertaker say to his girlfriend?

Em-balmy about you!

Did you hear about the vampire who died of a broken heart?

She had loved in vein.

What do girl snakes write on the bottom of their letters?

With love and hisses!

What did the
skeleton say to
his girlfriend?

*I love every bone in
your body!*

What feature do
witches love
on their
computers?

The spell-checker.

Who is
a vampire
likely to fall
in love with?

*The girl necks
door.*

James: *'I call my girlfriend Peach.'*

John: *'Because she's soft, and beautiful as a peach?'*

James: *'No, because she's got a heart of stone.'*

*'*I got a gold watch for my girlfriend.'

'I wish I could make a trade like that!'

So what did you trade for that?

GRANDAD

Witch: *'When I'm old and ugly, will you still love me?'*

Wizard: *'I do, don't I?'*

'**D**o you think, Professor, that my girlfriend should take up the piano as a career?'

'No, I think she should put down the lid as a favour!'

Their marriage was doomed from the start ...he wanted a cliffside wedding... she didn't...

What do you get when you cross a wedding with a cliff?

A marriage that is on the rocks.

First man: *'My girlfriend eats like a bird.'*

Second man: *'You mean she hardly eats a thing?'*

First man: *'No, she eats slugs and worms.'*

Did you hear about the monster who sent his picture to a lonely hearts club?

They sent it back, saying they weren't that lonely.

What does every girl have that she can always count on?

Fingers.

When you count to 10 using your fingers... Are you allowed to count your thumbs?

What happened when the snowman girl had a fight with her boyfriend?

She gave him the cold shoulder.

Every time I take my girlfriend out for a meal, she eats her head off.

She looks better that way.

First cannibal: *'My girlfriend's a tough old bird.'*

Second cannibal: *'You should have left her in the oven for another half-hour.'*

What did the wizard say to his witch girlfriend?

'Hello, gore-juice!'

Ooohh I hate it when he calls me gore-juice. It makes me sound like some kind of drink.

When Wally Witherspoon proposed to his girlfriend, she said, *'I love the simple things in life, Wally, but I don't want one of them for a husband!'*

What did the bull say to the cow?
'I'll love you for heifer and heifer.'

What do you call a hippo that believes in peace, love and understanding?

A hippie-potamus.

Who were the world's shortest lovers?
Gnomeo and Juliet.

Knock knock.

Who's there?

Ida.

Ida who?

Ida know why I love you like I do.

I can't understand
why people say my
girlfriend's legs look
like matchsticks.

*They do look like
sticks – but they
certainly don't match!*

What do you get when you cross
a vampire with a computer?

Love at first byte.

What Do You Call...

What do you call a dinosaur that never gives up?

A try and try and try-ceratops.

What do you call a man who shaves 15 times a day?

A barber.

It takes 15 shaves a day to keep my face as smooth as this. Oh...and a box of sticking plaster a bottle of antiseptic...and a good first aid kit...

What do you call an elephant that flies?

A jumbo jet.

What do you call a bee that buzzes quietly?

A mumble bee.

What do you call a cow that eats grass?

A lawn mooer.

What do you call a deer with only one eye?

No idea.

Boy! I'm finding it hard to keep up with the herd!

What do you call a deer with no legs and only one eye?

Still no idea.

What do arctic cows live in?

An igmoo.

What do you call a fish with no eyes?

Fsh.

What do you
call a messy cat?

Kitty litter.

Does KITTY have
no manners?

What do you
call a mosquito that
preters walking to flying?

An itch-hiker.

What do you call a pig that does karate?

Pork chop.

AAAARR-YA

Master Hog
demonstrating
his famous...
Pork Chop.

213

What do you call a pig who enjoys jumping from a great height?

A stydiver.

ERRRRR! WHAT A PIG!

What do you call a Russian fish?

A Tsardine.

What do you call an elephant that flies straight up?

An elecopter.

What do
you call a
pig with no
clothes on?

*Streaky
bacon.*

What do you call a well-behaved
goose?

A propaganda.

What do you
call a young
goat who visits
a psychiatrist?

A mixed-up kid.

What do you call a sheep in a bikini?

Bra-bra black sheep.

What do you call a shy sheep?

Baaaashful.

What do you call a tall building
that pigs work in?

A styscraper.

What do
you call
a zebra
without
stripes?

A horse.

HEY DON'T EAT ME! EAT THAT GUY!
DO YOU SEE ANY STRIPES
ON ME?
HE'S THE ZEBRA!

What do you call cattle that always sit down?

Ground beef.

What do you call the ghost of a chicken?

A poultrygeist.

What do you call two pigs who write letters to each other?

Pen-pals.

What do you call a man with a bus on his head?

Dead.

What do you call a bear with no fur?

A bare.

Sure it might be cool for a bear to shave all over and wear boxer shorts in summer... But let's just hope his fur grows back by Winter!

You're getting lazier and lazier...Pretty soon you're going to be fat...overweight and unhealthy!

I'd just die for a cup of coffee with four sugars!

What do you call a skeleton who sits around doing nothing?

Lazy bones.

What do you call a detective skeleton?

Sherlock Bones.

What do you call a witch without a broomstick?

A witch-hiker.

What do you call a hairy beast in a river?

A weir-wolf.

What do you call a protest march by devils?

A demon-stration.

What do you call banana skins that you wear on your feet?

Slippers.

What do you call two rows
of vegetables?

A dual cabbageway.

What do you
call a flea who
flies inside a
wally's head?

A space invader.

Well there's not
a lot of anything
inside there!

RATTLE CLUNK

What do you call the autobiography
of a shark?

A fishy story.

What do you call a wally with
half a brain?

A genius.